Secret Village
Winter

Thank you for choosing Ava Browne Coloring Books.
We strive to publish unique coloring books for all ages.

This coloring book contains double images, meaning you get to try different colors and shading for every page!!

If you found this coloring book enjoyable, please leave us a review.
Reviews help drive sales which allows us to make more coloring books.

www.avabrowne.com

This book also includes a free digital copy that you can print out at home. For instructions and your access code, please go to the last page.

Find us on social media:
facebook.com/groups/avabrownecoloring
https://www.instagram.com/ava_browne_coloring/

If you have any questions please contact us at:
Ava@avabrowne.com

Thank you and happy coloring!

COLOR TEST PAGE

COLOR TEST PAGE

DUPLICATE PAGES START HERE

WE PROVIDE DOUBLE PAGES SO CAN COLOR YOUR FAVORITE IMAGES TWICE USING DIFFERENT TECHNIQUES, SHARE WITH A FRIEND, OR REDO BECAUSE OF A MISTAKE.

DON'T FORGET TO VISIT AVABROWNE.COM TO DOWNLOAD YOUR FREE DIGITAL EDITION WHICH CAN BE PRINTED AND COLORED AS MANY TIMES AS YOU LIKE!

THE DOWNLOAD LINK AND PASSWORD ARE LOCATED ON THE LAST PAGE OF THIS BOOK.

Please visit

https://avabrowne.com/secret-village-winter-download/

to download your free digital copy.

Please consider subscribing to our newsletter, and enter the password

th2xn7q6

to access the file.(All Lowercase)

Made in United States
Orlando, FL
16 December 2024

55528706R00070